Proud of You!

You did such
a great job this week,
you get to
play dress-up!

_____
Date reward
was earned.

Spot-On Work!

You finished your homework early! This reward is good for a big hug!

_____

Date reward
was earned.

You're Terrific!

You're a superstar for doing extra work! This reward entitles you to stay up 30 minutes later tonight!

_____

Date reward was earned.

You Did It!

Wow, you rock!
For family movie night,
you get to pick
the movie!

_____
Date reward
was earned.

Super Worker!

You did a splendid job listening to your teacher! This reward is good for watching your favorite TV show tonight!

★ ★ ★ ★ ★

_____
Date reward was earned.

Marvelous Work!

You wowed us this week! This reward is good for one more bedtime story!

_____
Date reward was earned.

Keep It Up!

You were such
an amazing helper,
this reward entitles
you to one day
without chores!

_____

Date reward
was earned.

Good Work!

This reward entitles you to one hour of art time to draw, color, dance, or sing!

_____
Date reward
was earned.

Shine On!

You sat for a
whole call!
This reward entitles
you to 30 minutes
of extra TV time!

_____
Date reward
was earned.

Magnificent!

Grown-up: Write in your own special reward!

Date reward was earned.

Celebrate the fact that you're a rock star by going on an indoor treasure hunt!

_____

Date reward was earned.

Hooray!

You finished all your
work on time this week!
For family game night,
you get to pick
the game!

_____

Date reward
was earned.

You're Brilliant!

You reached your goal!
You get to go on
a scavenger hunt!

_____
Date reward
was earned.

You're Out of This World!

You did a marvelous job listening to instructions! This reward is good for wearing pajamas for a whole day!

_____
Date reward was earned.

Nicely Done!

You're terrific for taking your time on an assignment! Rock out with an instant dance party!

_____

Date reward was earned.

Amazing Job!

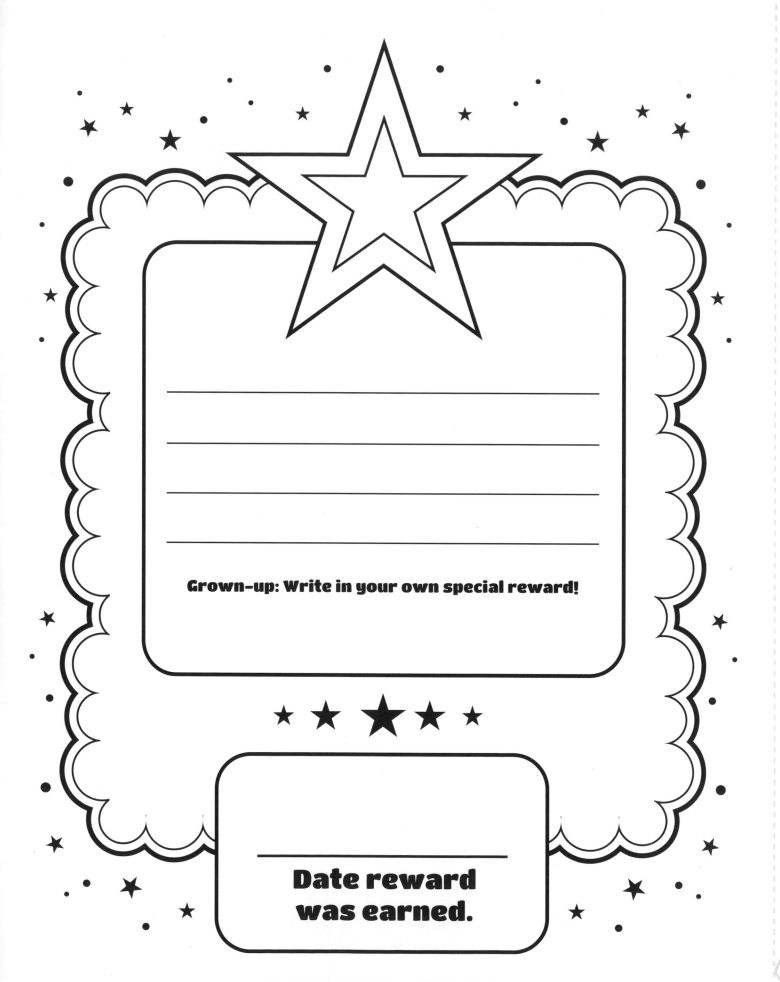

Grown-up: Write in your own special reward!

Date reward was earned.

Look Whooo's Great!

You were a brilliant listener this week! Cash in this reward to play family hide-n-seek!

_____

Date reward was earned.

Thumbs Up!

Thumbs up for
all your hard work!
You get to go on
a family walk!

Date reward
was earned.

You're Sssuper!

Your manners were so superb, this reward entitles you to build a fort!

★ ★ ★ ★ ★

_____
Date reward was earned.

Incredible Work!

Cash in this reward for extra bedtime hugs and kisses for the excellent work you did!

_____
Date reward
was earned.

Wonderful!

Grown-up: Write in your own special reward!

Date reward was earned.

Great Effort!

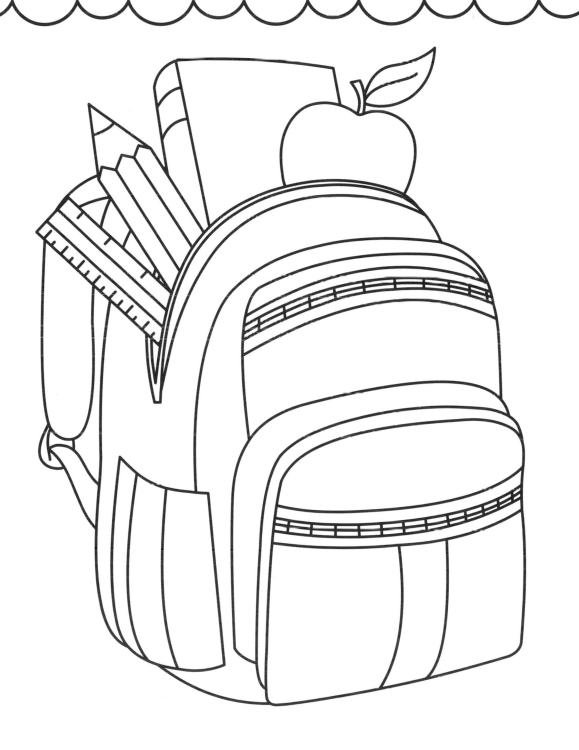

Your work was so impressive! You get to have a pillow fight!

_____
Date reward was earned.

Great Job!

This is a wild card for your stellar job this week: you get to choose any fun activity to do with the family!

_____
Date reward was earned.

Dazzling!

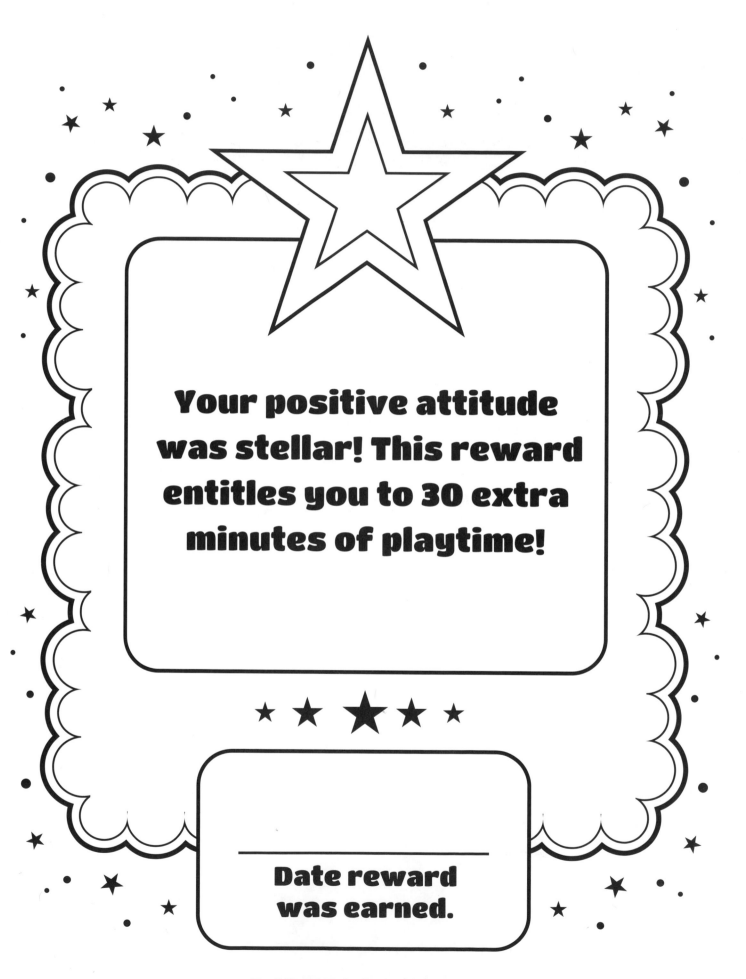

Your positive attitude was stellar! This reward entitles you to 30 extra minutes of playtime!

_____

Date reward was earned.

Sensational Job!

You were a super reader this week! You get to listen to music of your choice while working!

_____
Date reward was earned.

You Nailed It!

8 1 5 10

2 3 6 4

9 7

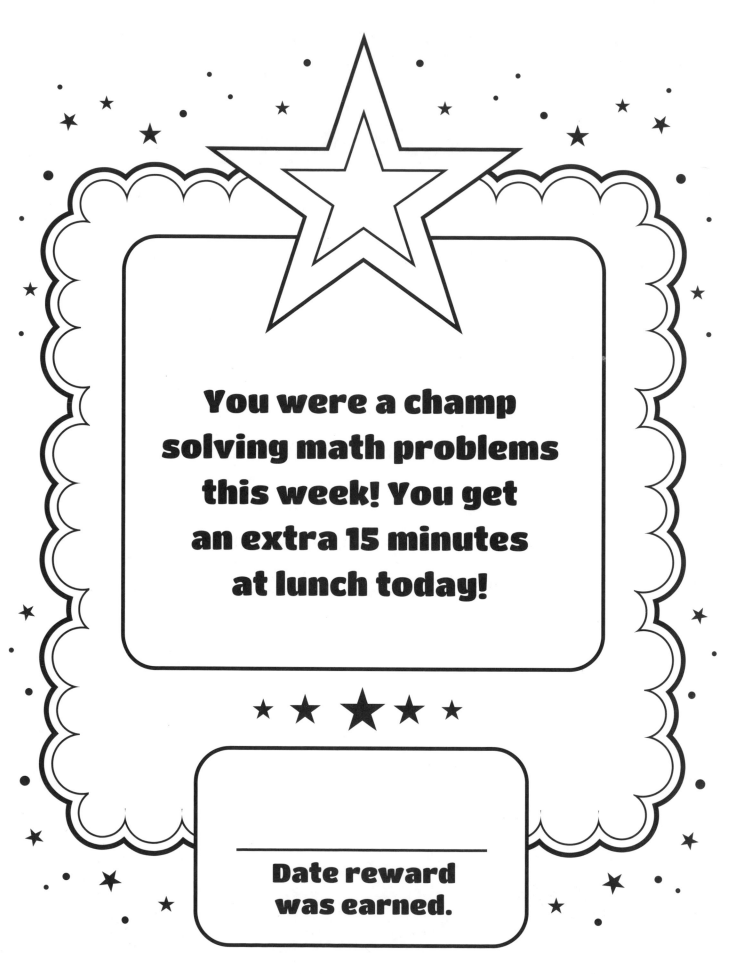

You were a champ solving math problems this week! You get an extra 15 minutes at lunch today!

_____
Date reward
was earned.

Superb!

You were so patient this week! You get to read your favorite bedtime story!

_____

Date reward
was earned.

Top-Notch Work!

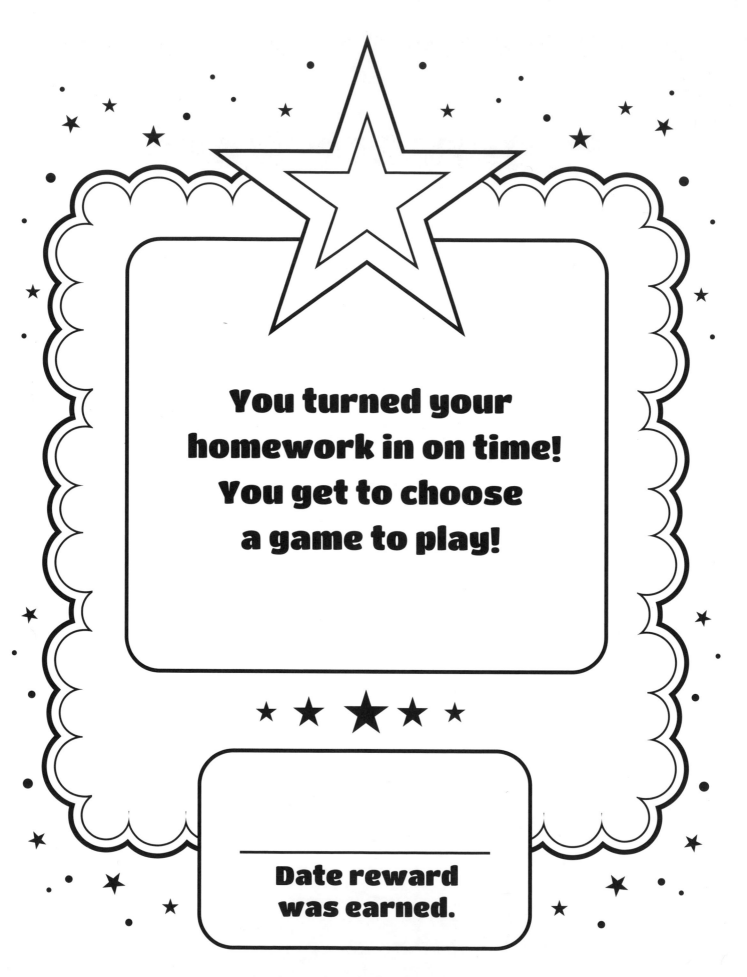

You turned your
homework in on time!
You get to choose
a game to play!

_____
Date reward
was earned.

Jump for Joy!

You did a terrific job
finishing your chores!
You get to
blow bubbles!

_____

Date reward
was earned.

Splendid!

This reward entitles you to choose any book to read out loud to the family!

_____
Date reward was earned.

Excellent!

You had some wonderful ideas! You get access to the remote control for an hour!

_____
Date reward was earned.

So Cool!

Cash in this reward to dance to your favorite song!

_____
Date reward was earned.

Terrific!

Your work was stellar this week! You get to be the family helper for the day!

_____

Date reward was earned.

You're a Rock Star!

You did your best work this week! You get to sing and dance to your favorite song!

_____
Date reward
was earned.

You're Paw-sitively Awesome!

Grown-up: Write in your own special reward!

_____ Date reward was earned.

You're a Champion Learner!

You get to choose a chore to skip for a day!

_____

Date reward was earned.

Remarkable!

You were so respectful this week! You get to watch your favorite movie tonight!

_____
Date reward was earned.

Fantastic Effort!

You started the day ready to learn! This reward is good for drawing a picture for 10 minutes!

_____
Date reward was earned.

Wow, You Rock!

Grown-up: Write in your own special reward!

Date reward
was earned.

You're Stellar!

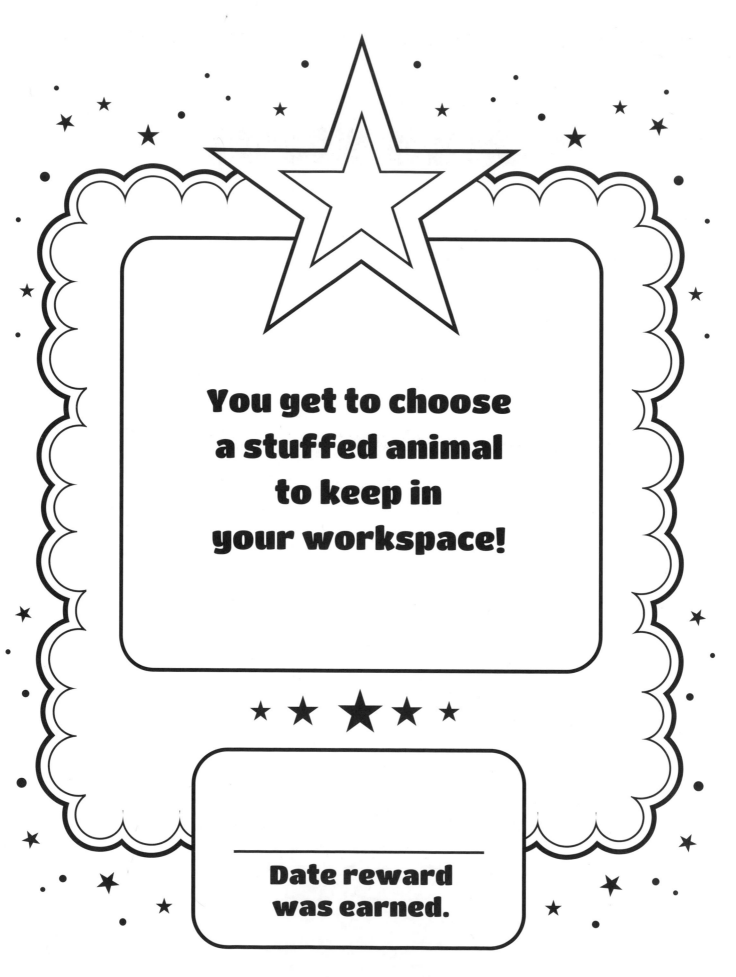

You get to choose
a stuffed animal
to keep in
your workspace!

_____

Date reward
was earned.

Well Done!

You did such an amazing
job cleaning up,
you get to choose
a family craft activity!

_____
Date reward
was earned.

Wow, You're Super!

This reward entitles you to dress up like a superhero for a day!

_____
Date reward was earned.

Awesome!

You're a rock star for sitting at the table to do work! You get to choose an extra special treat!

_____
Date reward was earned.

You're a Star!

You started school on time! This reward is good for telling jokes to the family!

★ ★ ★ ★ ★

_____
Date reward
was earned.

Spectacular Work!

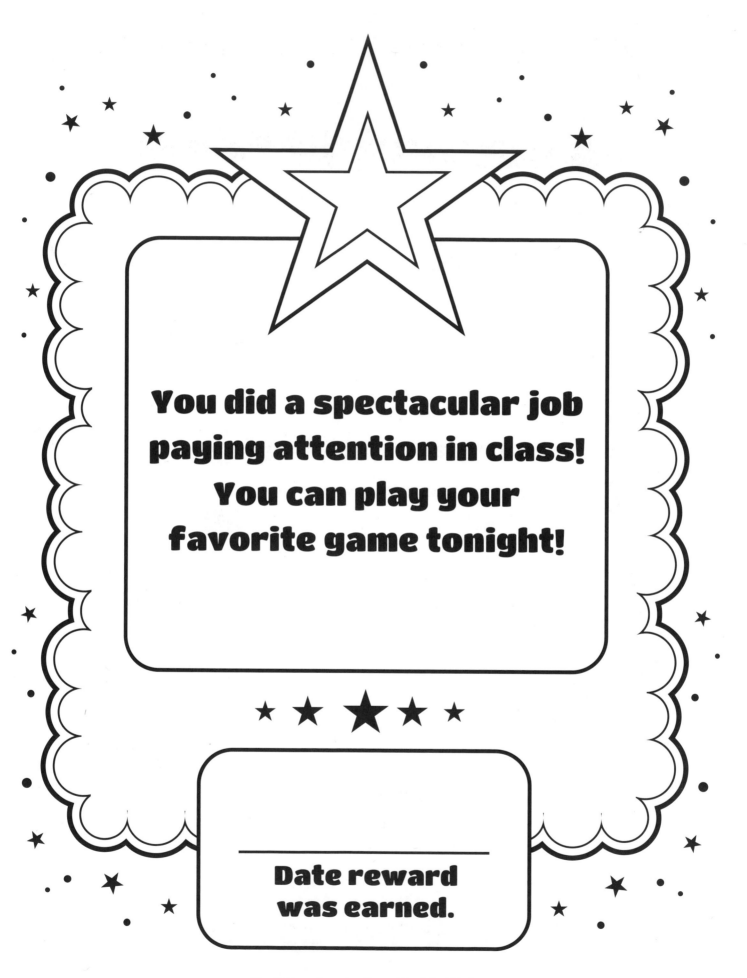

You did a spectacular job paying attention in class! You can play your favorite game tonight!

_____
Date reward
was earned.

Amazing Effort!

You made a lot of great progress! You get to sit in your favorite spot while working today!

_____

Date reward was earned.

Perfection!

Grown-up: Write in your own special reward!

Date reward was earned.

Outstanding!

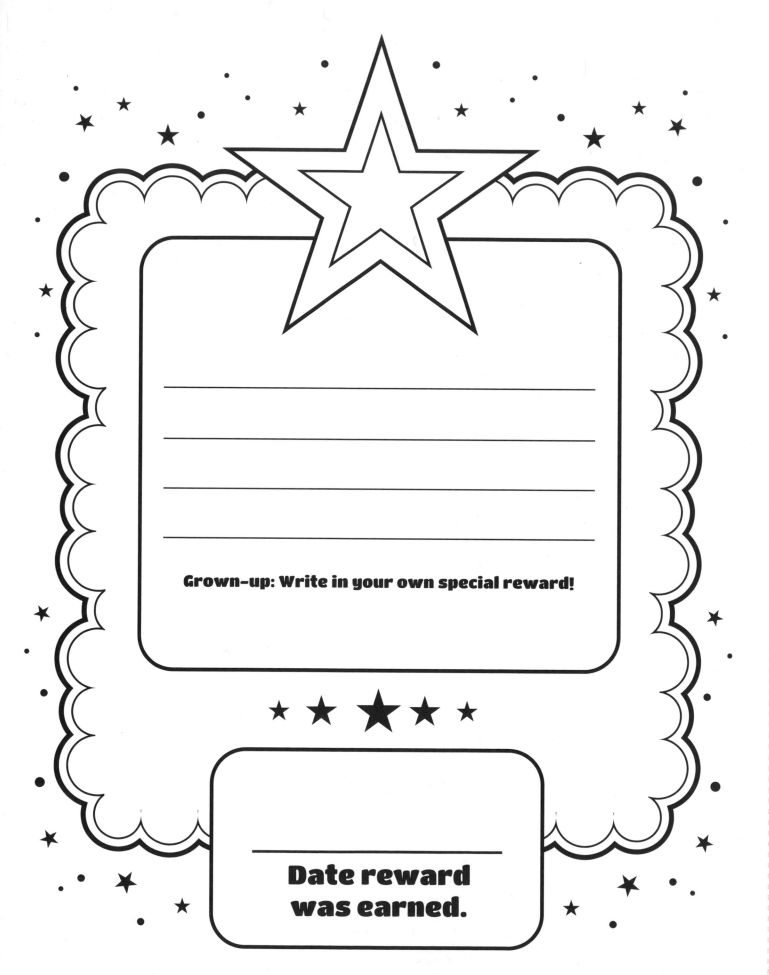

Grown-up: Write in your own special reward!

Date reward was earned.